Baby Animals! A Kid's Book of Amazing Pictures and Fun Facts About Baby Animals

By John Yost

Something Extra for You

ust to say "Thank you" for
rchasing this book, I want to give
ɔu a gift

100% absolutely free

Two beautiful "Baby Animal"
wallpapers you can use as
screensavers or as your desktop
background.

p://naturebooksforchildren.com/free-gift/

Table of Contents

Introduction

All animals have babies. Each baby needs to learn different things before it can go off on its own.

Parents teach their young many things to make sure their babies grow up to take care of themselves.

This baby elephant knows who its mother is and follows her by instinct.

ature also provides all animals
ith *instinct*. Instinct is something
ı animal knows at birth and never
ıs to learn.

ır example some monkeys never
ıve to learn to swim, they are
ırn knowing how to tread water.

But they do have to learn to watch out for crocodiles when they cross a river!

Human babies instinctively cry to communicate they need something, but they learn to speak so they can ask for what they want.

The length of time a baby stays with its parents depends on how long it takes for the baby to take care of itself. Some babies like whale calves stay with their mothers for two or three years. Other animals like baby wolf spiders leave their mom in a week.

Let's look at some different baby animals and see what makes them so interesting!

Baby Elephants

This baby elephant reaches for its mother's tail! It's like holding hands for elephants.

rican elephants are the world's
eaviest land animal. They are also
e second tallest animal in the
orld. (Can you guess the tallest
nimal in the world? You will find
ıt for sure later in this book!)

Before they are born, elephants develop in their mothers for 22 months. That's almost two years! Human babies only grow inside their mother for nine months.

Baby elephants are called *calves*. Sometimes two calves are born at the same time, but usually a mother elephant only has one baby.

Elephants weigh about 265 pounds when they are born, that's bigger than most adult people. They have a natural instinct to follow their mothers but since they don't see very well, they recognize their mom by the way she smells and by her voice.

lephants travel with the babies in the center of the herd to protect them from danger.

hen elephants are born, they on't know what to do with their unks. They swing them back and rth and sometimes even step on em! Some elephants suck their unks the way babies suck their umbs.

After about six months, the calves learn to control their trunks and can grab things with it.

Elephants are *mammals*. All mammals feed their babies milk to help them grow. A baby elephant drinks three gallons of milk every day!

In an elephant herd a baby elephant can get milk from any mother, but it usually goes to its own mom for milk.

Some elephant calves drink their mother's milk for nine years. That's a long time! They also eat bark, leaves, roots, grasses, and fruit.

Young female elephants that don't have babies of their own yet help

e mother elephants. They babysit
ne calves and make sure they don't
o too far from the rest of the herd.
nis helps teach the young females
ow to be good mothers when they
et older.

Baby Giraffes

This baby giraffe and its mother watch carefully to see if the people taking their picture are a threat.

Giraffes naturally live in Africa.

Baby giraffes are called *calves*. They grow in their mothers for about 1 1/2 years, before they are born.

14

When a baby giraffe is born, it drops six feet to the ground and lands on its head! This doesn't hurt the baby giraffe at all though.

Most giraffe mothers only have one calf, but sometimes twins are born. Giraffes are mammals, and the calves stand up and begin to drink milk from their mothers minutes after they are born.

During the day, the calves lie down to avoid being spotted by predators while the mother giraffes stay close by in case of danger. At night the baby stands up to drink its mother's milk before hiding in the grass again.

This mother giraffe nuzzles her calf after feeding it leaves.

When the calves can walk, all the mother giraffes herd their babies together into groups. The mothers take turns taking care of the calves and leaving the group to find food and water.

16

aby giraffes start eating plants at
nis time. If they can't reach high
 ough, the mother pulls leaves off
ne trees and feeds them to her
abies.

iraffes stop drinking their mother's
 ilk when they are about one year
 d and start eating plants. Thanks
  their mothers, they know what
 ants are good for them. Giraffes
 at leaves, flowers, seed-pods and
 uits.

 raffes can have babies of their
 vn when they are four years old.
 emale giraffes stay with the herd,
 it males leave to join a new group
  start their own herd.

Baby Kangaroos

This baby kangaroo, called a joey, is peeking out of its mother's pouch for the first time!

There are four different kinds of
kangaroos, and they all live in
Australia. Kangaroos are
marsupials. Marsupials are
mammals that carry their babies in
a pouch.

Baby kangaroos are called *joeys*.
Usually one joey is born at a time
but if there is a lot of food for the
mother, she might have two babies.

This baby kangaroo is coming out of its mom's pouch to eat some fresh grass.

Joeys are tiny when they are born. They are only the size of a grain of rice. It would take five newborn kangaroos to weigh as much as one nickel and each baby weighs less than a paper clip.

After a joey is born, it crawls up its mother's fur and into her pouch. The baby kangaroo stays in the pouch and drinks its mother's milk for a whole year, sometimes longer!

After about a year, the joey starts peeking out of its mother's pouch and soon after that it jumps out and eats grass and other plants.

Baby Lions

These lion cubs take a break from rough-housing with each other. Loins first learn to hunt and stalk by playing together.

The lion is known as the "King of the Beasts." Sometimes they are called the "King of the Jungle" but lions don't live in the jungle, they live on the plains of Africa.

group of lions is called a *pride*.
ale lions fight over who leads the
ide. The winning lion becomes the
ther to all the babies in the pride.

lioness can have up to six babies
one time. Newborn lion cubs
eigh between 2 and 4 pounds.
ney are too weak to walk their first
eek and their eyes don't open until
ey are 11 days old.

ne male lion's job is to protect the
ide. Only the mother lion takes
re of the cubs.

This cub gives its patient mother a big kiss.

Lion cubs drink milk for six months. Do you remember what an animal that drinks milk is called?   That's right! It's a mammal.

Sometimes mother lions have cubs that are born about the same time. When that happens, the mothers often share the job of raising the abies and they feed each others' ubs.

he cubs start to eat meat when hey are 3 months old. The mothers each the young lions to hunt, work gether and stay hidden.

ter about 2 1/2 years, male lions ave and go look for a pride they an take over. The young female ons stay with the pride their whole es and raise families of their own.

Baby Polar Bears

These polar bear cubs and their mother make their way to the ocean so the mother can hunt seals and feed her family.

Polar bears live on the ice in arctic regions around the North Pole. They are big, powerful white bears.

In autumn a mother polar bear uses her huge paws to dig a hole in the snow. She crawls in the snow den and stays there for 6-8 months. She doesn't eat, drink or go to the bathroom the whole time.

Polar bears have furry feet and special pads on their soles that keep them from slipping on the ice and snow.

After three months in the den, she usually has two bear *cubs*. Each cub is about the size of a stick of butter and has soft, fluffy fur. For the next four months the whole family stays in the den.

28

When the cubs come out of the den, they follow their mother to the edge of the ice where their mother hunts seals. She is very hungry after not eating for months!

For the next 2 1/2 years their mother teaches the cubs how to hunt, stay warm, and find shelter in one of the world's hardest places to survive. After that, the young bears go off on their own to hunt seals and start families.

Baby Purple Martins

These young purple martins can fly, but can't find their own food yet. These two wait in someone's backyard for their parents to bring them bugs.

Purple martins are birds that live in North and South America. They are

nown for their *migrations* where
ney fly long distances every year.

ney migrate north to be in the
arm Northern Hemisphere in April.
nen they turn around and travel
ack to South America in the fall
hen it gets cold.

urple martins breed when they fly
orth in the spring. The male finds
aves, grass, sticks, paper and
ud and gives it all to the female.
ne female uses what he brings to
uild a nest.

ne mother purple martin lays 3-8
nite, oval eggs. The mother and
ther take turns sitting on the eggs
keep them warm. In about 15

days the eggs hatch and the young martins demand lots of food.

This young purple martin opens its mouth wide hoping to get a treat from its father.

The baby that squawks the loudest and sticks its head up the highest gets the most to eat. That baby becomes the strongest and learns to fly first.

rple martins can fly after only one
onth in the nest but they don't
ow how to find their own food
t. The parents feed the babies for
e next 10 days while they teach
e young martins how to catch
gs and insects in midair.

rple martins even drink while
ing. They skim over a lake or
nd with their beak open and let
e water rush in.

e family stays together all
mmer. In the fall the young
artins are strong enough to fly all
e way to South America with their
others.

Baby Rabbits

This baby rabbit nibbles grass and flowers while keeping an eye out for danger.

Rabbits live in many parts of the world. Wild rabbits live in underground holes called *burrows*.

Rabbits are popular with humans because they make cute pets. But unless you have a big cage, it's not a good idea to get a rabbit.

aby rabbits are called *kits* or *unnies*. There are usually six kits in litter. That is a lot of babies! Since any animals eat rabbits, having a t of babies makes it more likely at some of them will live to be dults.

Bunnies are blind and helpless when they are born. They can't find their own food. It's okay though, they drink their mother's milk.

The milk has everything the babies need to stay healthy and grow fast. After only one month, the kits can walk and feed on their own.

Kits stay close to their burrow until they learn to run fast. That way they can get to the burrow quickly if a predator comes.

Rabbits are *herbivores*. Herbivores are animals that only eat plants. The baby rabbits eat all parts of a lant including the stems, flowers, eeds and even roots.

Baby Raccoons

This sleepy baby raccoon pokes its head out of the den to see what's going on outside.

Raccoon mothers usually only have one litter each year. She gives birth to 3-7 baby raccoons, called *yearlings*.

The mother raccoon chooses a den that is safe for her babies. Often raccoon dens are in holes of trees or big piles of rocks.

The yearlings stay in the den for two months before they can find food on their own. Raccoons are very curious, and once they are out of the den, they investigate *everything*. Sometimes they get themselves into trouble!

This baby raccoon's mom will teach it to balance on small trees so it doesn't get hurt.

Young raccoons stay with their mother for a year while she teaches them how to run, climb, and find food. Some people think that raccoons wash their food, but they are really feeling around for food underwater.

When the baby raccoons grow up and have families of their own, they usually try to find a place close to their mother's den.

In cities raccoons can become pests because they often raid bird feeders and dig through people's garbage looking for food.

Baby Sea Turtles

This tiny sea turtle makes cute little tracks through the sand on its way to the water.

There are seven species of sea turtles, and they are found in every ocean except the Arctic Ocean.

other sea turtles make 2-5 nests each year and lay over 100 eggs in each nest! That's a lot of eggs!

To make a nest the mother uses her flippers like big shovels to dig a hole in the sand. She knows to make her nest above where the cold water comes at high tide. The mother sea turtle lays her eggs and then covers them up with sand.

Hundreds of sea turtles hatch from eggs all at once and hurry to the ocean.

The mother sea turtle doesn't have to sit on her eggs like the purple martin because the sand keeps her eggs warm.

Baby sea turtles usually hatch at night to avoid predators. Instinct tells the young hatchlings to head

r water. The baby turtles suddenly
ring from the nest and waddle to
e ocean.

nce in the water, the baby turtles
de in seaweed, where they find
a-plants and little animals to eat.

*his turtle is about to be let go in the ocean
ter being cared for by people who help save
sea turtles.*

Many of the hatchlings are eaten by birds and fish but since there are so many babies, some of them survive.

The biggest problem adult sea turtles have is getting caught in underwater fishing nets. Turtles can't breathe underwater, so they drown in the nets.

Some people who like sea turtles are trying to make these nets illegal so the turtles don't die. Other people help the young turtles get stronger before letting them go in the wild.

Baby Tigers

Tigers are born with blue eyes but as the cubs get older, their eyes turn yellow.

48

Tigers are the biggest species in the cat family, even bigger than lions! They live in Russia, China, Korea, India and the Himalayan Mountains. There are lots of tigers at the zoo, and you might see one there.

Mother tigers usually have one or two babies (called *cubs*), but sometimes they have seven babies at once! The babies have beautiful blue eyes when they are young.

Newborn tiger cubs are blind, helpless and very small. They only weigh about as much as a quart of milk. The cubs' eyes don't open until they are one or two weeks old.

This mother tiger takes her cub to a safer place. It doesn't hurt tiger cubs to be carried this way.

Tigers are mammals, and like all mammals they drink milk from their mothers. The mother tiger spends most of her time with her cubs right after they are born.

When the cubs are about two-months old, they start eating meat from animals their mother kills. When the cubs are five or six months old, they join her on hunting trips. Their mother teaches them how to stalk and catch monkeys, deer, antelope and even fish!

Tiger cubs stay with their mothers learning everything they can until they are two or three years old. Then they go away to live on their own.

Baby Whales

This painting shows a mother humpback whale and her calf swimming together on their way to Alaska.

The biggest animal to ever live on earth is the blue whale. They even are bigger than the biggest dinosaur.

Whales are mammals that live in the ocean. Unlike fish, whales have to come to the surface of the water for air. They don't breathe through their mouths like we do though. They breathe through a special hole on top of their head called a *blowhole*.

Did you know that a baby whale can't swim for 30 minutes after it's born? The whale's mother holds her baby up out of the water so the baby can breathe until it can swim to the surface on its own.

This beluga whale calf taps its mother's stomach so mom knows it's hungry.

Baby blue whales are the biggest babies in the world. They weigh more than a Smart Car when they are born! They grow fast too, and gain 200 pounds *every day for a year*.

The young calves drink their mother's milk for their first 2 years.

54

You might think it's hard to drink milk underwater, especially since baby whales don't have lips. What happens is that the baby nudges its mother's stomach to let her know is hungry. Then the mom squirts milk right into her baby's open mouth!

The mother needs a lot of food to make all that milk. So, the young calf has to swim hundreds of miles with its mother as she goes to better feeding grounds.

Baby Wolf Spiders

Do you see something strange about this spider? If you look closely, you'll notice that there are tiny baby spiders on her back.

Wolf spiders mate in the spring and the mother lays her eggs inside a bag she makes out of web. The bag is called an *egg sac*. There are more than 100 baby spiders in an egg

ac. She carries the egg sac around
ith her and even hunts carrying
e heavy load.

hen the eggs are ready to hatch,
e mother splits the bag open so
er babies can get out. The baby
piders scramble up their mother's
ack one on top of the other in
yers. They ride on their mother's
ack and she protects them from
anger.

These newly hatched wolf spiders climb on their mother's back. She protects them until they can survive on their own.

But after only a week the babies can take care of themselves and they go off on their own to find food.

Wolf spiders are carnivores and like lions and tigers they only eat meat. But wolf spiders prey on small

sects and bugs, not wildebeest
d antelope!

Wrapping up

As you can see, there are a lot of different baby animals in the world and each of them has different things to learn before they can take care of themselves.

Isn't it amazing how different animals learn to solve the problems they have growing up? They have to learn a lot on their own, but their parents guide and teach them so they can take care of themselves.

A Note From John

ear Reader,

hank you very much for reading
y book on baby animals. I get
eat feedback from teachers,
arents and children who have
njoyed this book. I hope you liked
too!

you did, please leave a 5 Star
view on Amazon. Your review
ally helps me out a lot and is the
obably the most appreciated thing
u can do for me! :) You can
ave your review by going to your
nazon account and clicking on
ur *Baby Animals* book.

by Animals is the second in a
ries of *Nature Books for Children*

that I'm researching and writing. Every time I write a book, I'm fascinated by what I learn. For example I had no idea that a baby giraffe falls 6 feet and hits its head on the ground when it's born. Or that kangaroos start out only as big as a grain of sand. Nature is just so cool!

It's my hope that I can pass some of my love and enthusiasm for nature on to you and your children.

I also write in hopes that your family enjoys reading these books and talking about them together; giving you the opportunity to teach strong values to your children and grow closer as a family.

d of course, I truly hope you are
spired to appreciate this beautiful
orld we live in.

gain, if you and your children have
njoyed this book, I'd like to ask
ou to leave a great review on
mazon. Reviews help others
scover the book and I love
nowing that I've given something
 you and your family.

ank you so much!

hn

S. Feel free to write me to chat,
ve me ideas for new books, or tell
e how I can make them better for
u and your family. You can email
e at johnnie.yost@gmail.com

Thanks again!

P.P.S. Please visit my author page below to see what new books you and your kids can enjoy together!

http://amazon.com/author/johnyost

Photography Credits:

ese people were kind enough to let
hers use their photographs, the least
e can do is show them we appreciate
eir work and kindness. Images in
der of appearance (If an image isn't
ted here, that means I purchased the
hts to it):

ont cover – DigitalART2@flickr.com

lar Bear cub between mother's legs -
rilop311@flickr.com

bbit kit in grass and daisy fleabane –
taylor@stockexchng

ue-eyed tiger cub –
rgersZoo@fliker.com

seup of Wolf spider and babies –
kimedia.org

Made in the USA
Las Vegas, NV
03 December 2021